May your Mother's Day make you
smile and your heart blossom.

Godmothers are special...

they are chosen.

Only a Godmother can...

Give hugs like a mother,

Can keep secrets like a sibling,

And share love like a friend!

A Godmother always has love

to give and time to spare.

A Godmother is always there.

You are one fabulous Godmother!

You are one fabulous Godmother!

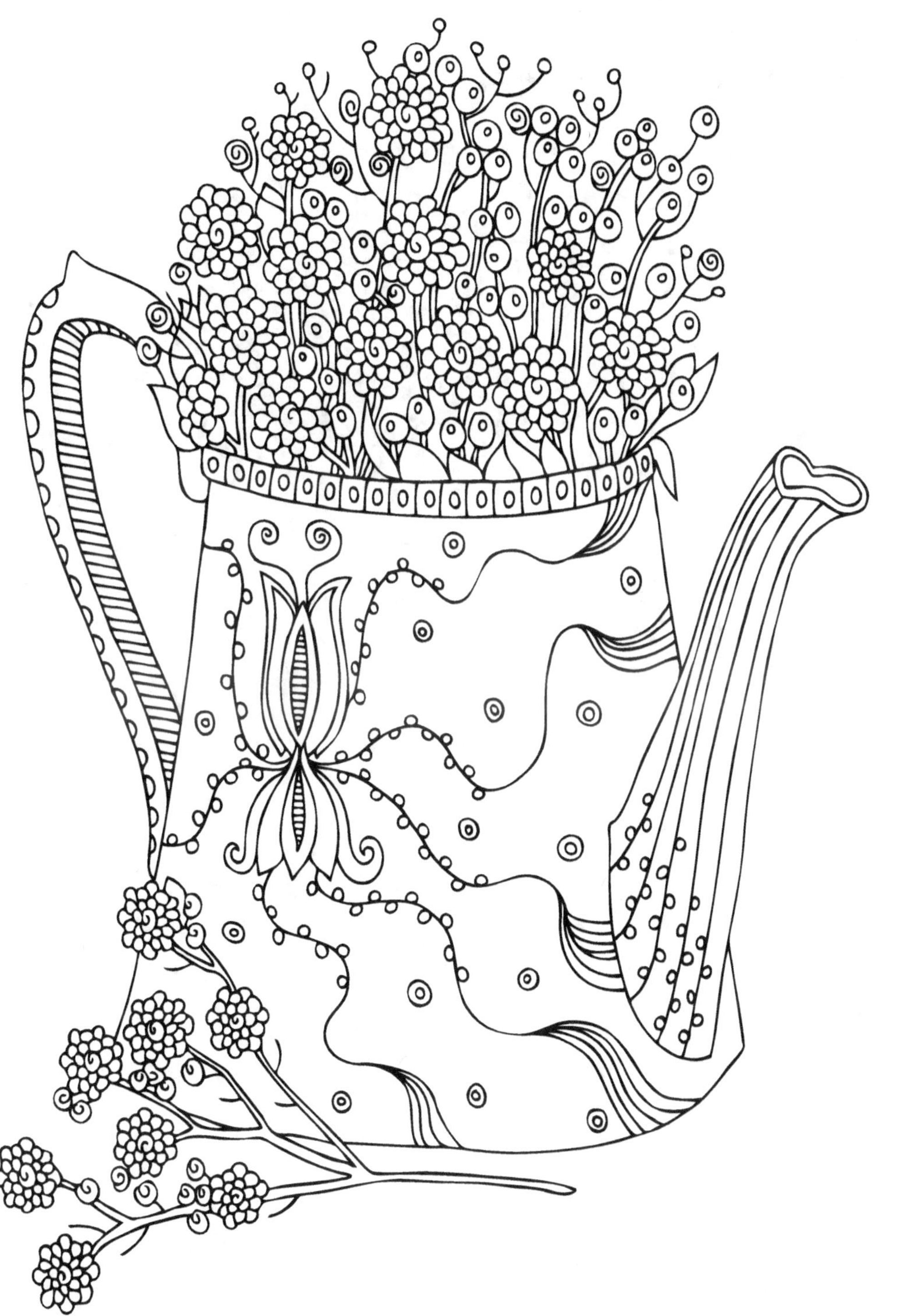

May your Mother's Day be as bright
and beautiful as you are!

You are always in my heart!

You are always in my heart!

LOVE

Godmothers are precious people
who cause joyful happenings in the
hearts of children.

Every day is special with a Godmother like you!

You are the best Godmother ever!

You do small things with great love!
Saint Theresa

May all of your dreams come true!

May all of your dreams come true!

LOVE
PARIS
bonjour

flowers for your special day!

Wishing you a day that is
just like you want it to be!

Happy Mother's Day to a
Wonderful Godmother!
(Coloring Card)
Copyright 2018

Sending you love, wishes, and blessings on
Mother's Day!

From,

_________________________________________________